The Inner Thoughts of an Eccentric English Teacher

Rose Spino-Stahl

BookLeaf
Publishing

The Inner Thoughts of an Eccentric English Teacher © 2023 Rose Spino-Stahl

Presentation by *BookLeaf Publishing*

Web: www.bookleafpub.com

E-mail: info@bookleafpub.com

ISBN: 9789357212816

First edition 2023

To my students, past, present, and future, this one is for you.

ACKNOWLEDGEMENT

I would like to thank Book Leaf Publishing who challenged my writing process and pushed me pass my limitations.

I would also like to thank my parents for always cheering in my corner and my hubby for believing in me through all my crazy ideas.

Without them, this book would not have been possible.

PREFACE

You are about to discover just a few inner thoughts of a High School English teacher. The good and the bad. These poems are inspired by my real teaching experiences. Enjoy.

Hard

Alarm buzz clock alarm buzz clock gotta get up five more minutes gotta get up don't want to get up but must get up shower hair brush teeth pet dog pack lunch no time for breakfast sign in have to cover day already shot ten minutes left to set my board up what are we doing today standards up date up kids come in hello hello hello welcome glad you're here good morning grunt smiles actually got a reply hello hello hello bell rings teaching begins this one is watching the latest episode of a teen drama I haven't seen that one yet can't watch I don't want to spoil it that one is playing pool that one is in foster care that one just got stabbed in a fight that one got jumped by her ex okay let's talk Shakespeare why are you guys not listening duh how can I make this more interactive more fun engaging why is admin walking into my room observations observing not one not two but four people in my room to check to see what we are doing why are you reading Shakespeare how will they know when I don't even know this isn't going to go well lockdown lockdown lockdown this doesn't seem planned close the blinds shut the lights make sure the lights are off calm

thirty-five teenagers and four admin don't lose
your composer keep it together huddle together
be quiet be silent
BANG
If that was hard to read, think how hard it is for a
teacher.

The Start of the Year Haiku

It is almost time,
To unpack stuff and say hi.
Another school year to start.

The ABCs of Teaching

Attendance
Books
Calendars
Discovery
Electronics
Foreshadowing
Geometry
History
Intelligence
Journey
Kids
Learning
Mathematics
Negotiating
Opportunity
Productivity
Quality
Respect
Supportive
Teaching
Understanding
Vocabulary
Wondering
Xerox
Youth
Zilch

Ticonderoga

One by one they sharpen their pencil
Because it broke on their paper
In it goes. It is so suspenseful.
Is it real or a faker?

Around it goes. We hear the break.
Around it goes again until it becomes a nub
Why do they make...
Them awful? Hope they aren't used in a Golf
club.

They may cost an extra dime.
Expect nothing less superior
But they are the greatest of all time.
Why bother with the inferior?

They wear the toga!
They are the best. Ticonderoga

Last Year

Hello.
Do you remember me?
I was in your class last year.
I know I wasn't the easiest.
Never wanted to be here.
Always getting into trouble.
But I want you to know
You were my favorite teacher.
I know you pushed me to succeed.
I know you only wanted the best for me.
You called my Grandma
Told her how I did so well.
She was proud of me.
I was proud of myself.
I remember when you told me
My grade. I smiled.
A huge grin.
I'm sorry I didn't show
my appreciation more.
I was just a kid last year.
I wanted to stop by and say hi.
Let you know, that I thank you
For all the care you shared
I might not smile at you in the halls.
I might ignore you when you call.

But know I'm grateful everyday
That I got to sit in room 514.

Why?

Why do I teach?
Do I make a difference?
Do I empower?
Or do I enable?
Do I push too hard?
Or not enough?
Heroes... society thinks of us.
School boards refuse to pay us.
Parents blame us.
Students disrespect us.
Why do I teach?
Is it for the summers,
Filled with trainings?
Is it the breaks,
Filled with planning?
Do they know how much I care?
Do they know I want them to succeed?
Do they know why I push them,
Because I know they can succeed?
Why are some days harder then others?
Why do I always question,
My yearning to teach?

I Cried Today

I cried today.
Not because I was sad,
But because I care.
I sympathize too much.

I cried today.
Not because I am weak,
But because I wear my emotions.
I feel too much.

I cried today.
Not because of any one event,
But because I don't feel valued.
I think too much.

Sunday Nights

I watch as the clock ticks on
My mind racing with thoughts of tomorrow
Will my students show up?
Will they be late?
Will they care about the lesson?
I go through the motions of
Washing clothes
Meal prepping
Netflixing
But my mind continues to race with thoughts of
tomorrow

She Don't Teach Us

Good morning!
No.
I'm so excited about today!
No.
I've worked so hard on this lesson!
No.
You're going love it!
No.
Please turn to page 36.
No.
Why are you up?
No.
Please sit down.
No.
Are you watching videos on your phone?
No.
Are you listening to what I say?
No.
I give up.
No.
Are you going to do the work?
No.
Then I'm not sure what to do.

Prepared

Does my smile
Hide my dark circles?
The fact that I
Stayed up all night.
Mind racing
Of thoughts of the week.
Will I be able to
Get things ready?
Of course.
I always do.

The Hats We Wear...

Educator
Record keeper
Secretary
Nurse
Data tracker
Phycologist
Therapist
Referee
Consistency
Advocate
Cheerleader
Teacher

Coffee

The magic bean
That gets me through the day.
The liquid spark
This enchanted cup of bliss
The extraordinary energy
It exudes
My one
My only
Saving grace

Friday Night Fun

Red
White
Dry
Sweet
Acidity
Aroma
Balance
Aging
Blend
Brilliant
Brut
Complex
Cork
Earthy
Foxy
Fruity
Flavors
Glass
Bottle
Tasting
Barrel
All
Of
The
Above

Plans of Fantasy

Saturday...
I will...
Vacuum
Clean
Laundry
Cook
Lessons
Grading
Reality...
I did...
Absolutely
Nothing
And
Loved
It

A Team

The people that have your back
The ones you can air out your frustrations
The ones that listen to you vent
The ones you lean on
The ones you laugh with
The ones you pick up
More then a team
More then friends
More like family

That One Kid

You know that one kid
The one that annoys everyone
Even the students sometimes

You know that one kid
That you have a soft spot for
Cuz you see so much potential?

You know that one kid
That makes you laugh
But also makes you cry.

You know that one kid
That's going through a lot
But hides it with outbursts.

You know that one kid
That just needs to be loved
But asks it in the most harsh ways.

Yeah, we all have that one kid.

May

Since August I have been with these kids.
I've seen
love blossom
And heartbreak collide.
I've seen
Set backs
And great growth.
I've seen
Lessons learned
That no test can measure.
I've seen
The spark of knowledge
Set forth in their eyes.
I've seen
Some leave
And other come back.
I've seen
What the future holds
And it sets them free.
I will miss them but hope they remember this
time we shared.

An End of the Year Haiku

It is almost time,
To pack up and say goodbye.
One more school year done.

Rumors

Have you heard about that teacher?
She's in room 514.
I heard she always smiles
Even when she's irate.
Some students think she's faking
Like it's all just one facade.
But I've seen her in the hallways,
She's always cheerful and bright.
She wears all those interesting outfits
And those earrings are always a sight.
We should sign up for her class.
To see if the rumors
about her
are the real deal.

My Great Escape

No alarm clocks to wake me
from my slumber
Yet, I'm still up before dawn

Rope drop calling
my name

The castle
I wish to see

The mouse
I long to hug

It's childish they say
And I embrace my inner child everyday

This is my time
My time to be free

My time
to enjoy

My time
to have fun

And make memories

This is my great escape

Going Back

A few weeks away.
Anxiety creeps near.
But I've prepared all summer
For this moment.
I have all my icebreakers planned.
All lessons are engaging.
Even used the district curriculum
Because of course they won't change it.

The phones rings.
It's my colleague.

Have I heard?
They changed the curriculum?
I'm not teaching what they told me?
All my planning was for nothing?
All my planning was for nothing.

Hours of unpaid time.
Another year of something new.
Embracing it with smiles
...
and prayers.